EMMANUEL JOSEPH

The Weight of Wealth, How Billionaires Navigate Power, Purpose, and Humanity

Copyright © 2025 by Emmanuel Joseph

All rights reserved. No part of this publication may be reproduced, stored or transmitted in any form or by any means, electronic, mechanical, photocopying, recording, scanning, or otherwise without written permission from the publisher. It is illegal to copy this book, post it to a website, or distribute it by any other means without permission.

First edition

This book was professionally typeset on Reedsy.
Find out more at reedsy.com

Contents

1 Chapter 1: The Pinnacle of Power 1
2 Chapter 2: The Purposeful Path 3
3 Chapter 3: Humanity and the Rich 5
4 Chapter 4: The Double-Edged Sword of Success 7
5 Chapter 5: Philanthropy and Its Discontents 9
6 Chapter 6: The Global Influence 11
7 Chapter 7: The Ethical Dilemmas 13
8 Chapter 8: The Legacy of Wealth 15
9 Chapter 9: The Burden of Wealth 16
10 Chapter 10: The Role of Innovation 17
11 Chapter 11: The Power of Networks 19
12 Chapter 12: The Art of Delegation 21
13 Chapter 13: The Intersection of Wealth and Politics 23
14 Chapter 14: The Balancing Act 25
15 Chapter 15: The Influence of Technology 27
16 Chapter 16: The Dynamics of Family Wealth 29
17 Chapter 17: The Future of Wealth 31

1

Chapter 1: The Pinnacle of Power

In the world of the ultra-rich, power isn't just a byproduct of wealth; it's the very essence of influence. Billionaires often find themselves in a unique position where their financial clout can sway governments, shape industries, and redefine societal norms. This chapter explores the dynamics of power among the super-wealthy, examining how they wield it to achieve their goals and the ethical considerations that come with such immense influence. From boardrooms to political arenas, the decisions made by these individuals have far-reaching consequences that ripple through every stratum of society.

The weight of this power is immense, and with it comes a responsibility that few can truly comprehend. Some billionaires use their influence for the greater good, funding philanthropic initiatives and advocating for social change. Others, however, may prioritize personal gain, exploiting loopholes and exerting pressure to maintain their status. The fine line between benevolent leadership and ruthless ambition often blurs, raising questions about the true nature of power and its impact on humanity.

This chapter delves into the psychology of power, exploring how it shapes the behavior and decisions of billionaires. It examines the temptations and pitfalls that come with immense influence, highlighting the importance of self-awareness and ethical considerations. Through interviews and case studies, readers gain insight into the minds of the world's most powerful individuals and the internal struggles they face.

Ultimately, the chapter encourages readers to reflect on their own relationship with power and influence. It challenges them to consider how they would navigate similar circumstances and the ethical dilemmas that arise. By understanding the complexities of power, readers can gain a deeper appreciation for the responsibilities that come with great wealth and influence.

2

Chapter 2: The Purposeful Path

While power is an undeniable aspect of wealth, purpose is what truly gives it meaning. This chapter explores how billionaires find and define their purpose, often through philanthropic endeavors and impactful projects. From building schools in impoverished regions to funding groundbreaking research, the ultra-rich have the resources to make a significant difference in the world. However, their motivations can vary widely, from genuine altruism to strategic reputation building.

The search for purpose is a deeply personal journey, influenced by an individual's values, experiences, and worldview. Some billionaires are driven by a desire to leave a lasting legacy, while others are motivated by a sense of duty to give back. This chapter examines the different ways in which billionaires define their purpose and the impact of their actions on society.

Through a series of inspiring stories and examples, readers are introduced to billionaires who have made a positive difference in the world. From environmental conservation to education and healthcare, these individuals have dedicated their wealth to causes that align with their values. The chapter also explores the challenges and criticisms they face, including accusations of using philanthropy as a means of self-promotion.

Ultimately, this chapter encourages readers to reflect on their own sense of purpose and how they can make a positive impact in their own lives. It highlights the importance of aligning one's actions with their values and the potential for creating meaningful change, regardless of one's financial status.

3

Chapter 3: Humanity and the Rich

Despite their wealth and influence, billionaires are still human, with their own struggles, insecurities, and desires. This chapter delves into the personal lives of the ultra-rich, exploring how they balance their public personas with their private realities. It examines the challenges they face in maintaining genuine relationships, raising families, and finding happiness amidst their immense responsibilities.

The weight of wealth can take a toll on an individual's mental and emotional well-being. Billionaires often find themselves isolated, surrounded by people who may have ulterior motives or who treat them differently because of their status. This chapter explores the emotional and psychological impact of immense wealth, shedding light on the often-overlooked human side of the ultra-rich.

Through personal anecdotes and interviews, readers gain insight into the daily lives of billionaires and the unique challenges they face. The chapter also examines the coping mechanisms they use to manage stress and maintain their mental health. From therapy and meditation to hobbies and creative pursuits, billionaires find various ways to navigate the pressures of their extraordinary lives.

Ultimately, this chapter humanizes the ultra-rich, reminding readers that, despite their immense wealth, they are still subject to the same emotions and struggles as everyone else. It encourages readers to approach the topic of wealth with empathy and understanding, recognizing the complexities and nuances of the human experience.

4

Chapter 4: The Double-Edged Sword of Success

Success, while often celebrated, comes with its own set of challenges and dilemmas. This chapter explores the double-edged sword of success, examining how billionaires navigate the pressures and expectations that come with their achievements. It delves into the sacrifices they make, the failures they encounter, and the resilience required to maintain their status.

The pursuit of success can be all-consuming, often requiring immense dedication and hard work. Billionaires are no strangers to long hours, relentless pressure, and high stakes. This chapter highlights the personal sacrifices they make, including time spent away from family and the toll on their health and well-being. It also explores the resilience and determination that drive them to overcome obstacles and achieve their goals.

Success also brings with it heightened expectations and scrutiny. Billionaires often find themselves under the public eye, their actions and decisions closely watched and judged. This chapter examines the pressure to maintain their success and the fear of failure that looms over them. It also explores the role of public perception and the strategies billionaires use to manage their image and reputation.

Ultimately, this chapter challenges readers to reconsider their own definitions of success and the sacrifices they are willing to make in its pursuit. It encourages them to reflect on the balance between ambition and well-being, and the importance of resilience and self-care.

5

Chapter 5: Philanthropy and Its Discontents

Philanthropy is often seen as a noble endeavor, but it is not without its controversies and criticisms. This chapter delves into the complexities of billionaire philanthropy, examining the motivations behind their charitable efforts and the impact on society. It explores the fine line between genuine altruism and strategic self-interest, and the ethical dilemmas that arise.

Billionaires have the resources to make a significant difference in the world, and many choose to do so through philanthropy. This chapter highlights the various causes they support, from education and healthcare to environmental conservation and social justice. It also examines the different approaches they take, including direct donations, foundation grants, and impact investing.

However, philanthropy is not without its challenges and criticisms. Some argue that billionaire philanthropy can perpetuate inequality and concentrate power in the hands of a few. Others question the motivations behind charitable efforts, accusing billionaires of using philanthropy as a means of self-promotion or tax avoidance. This chapter explores these debates and the ethical considerations involved.

Ultimately, this chapter encourages readers to reflect on the role of philanthropy in society and the responsibilities that come with immense wealth. It challenges them to consider the impact of their own charitable efforts and the importance of genuine altruism and ethical decision-making.

6

Chapter 6: The Global Influence

The reach of billionaires extends far beyond their immediate surroundings, impacting global economies and shaping international policies. This chapter explores the ways in which the ultra-rich exert their influence on a global scale, from investments in emerging markets to lobbying for favorable trade agreements. It examines the complexities of navigating international relations and the ethical considerations that arise when personal interests intersect with global concerns.

Billionaires often have the resources and connections to influence international policies and decisions. This chapter highlights the various ways in which they leverage their wealth and power to shape the global landscape. It also explores the challenges they face in balancing their personal interests with the greater good and the impact of their actions on different communities and countries.

Through case studies and interviews, readers gain insight into the strategies and motivations behind the global influence of billionaires. The chapter also examines the role of multinational corporations and the ways in which billionaires use their businesses to drive change on a global scale. From philanthropy to political lobbying, the ultra-rich have the ability to make a significant impact on the world stage.

Ultimately, this chapter encourages readers to consider the broader implications of wealth and power on a global scale. It challenges them to reflect on the responsibilities that come with immense influence and the importance of ethical decision-making in the face of complex global issues.

7

Chapter 7: The Ethical Dilemmas

Wealth and power often come with a myriad of ethical dilemmas, forcing billionaires to confront difficult decisions and moral quandaries. This chapter delves into the ethical challenges faced by the ultra-rich, exploring how they navigate issues such as tax avoidance, corporate responsibility, and social justice. It examines the role of personal values and the impact of public scrutiny on their decision-making processes.

The ethical dilemmas faced by billionaires are often multifaceted and complex. This chapter highlights the various ways in which they grapple with these challenges, from making decisions that prioritize profit over people to addressing the social and environmental impacts of their actions. It also explores the influence of public perception and the ways in which billionaires manage their reputations in the face of ethical controversies.

Through interviews and real-life examples, readers gain insight into the ethical considerations that shape the behavior of billionaires. The chapter also examines the role of corporate social responsibility and the ways in which billionaires use their businesses to address ethical issues. From environmental sustainability to labor practices, the ultra-rich have the ability to drive change and set new standards for ethical behavior.

Ultimately, this chapter encourages readers to reflect on their own ethical values and the importance of integrity in decision-making. It challenges them to consider how they would navigate similar ethical dilemmas and the impact of their actions on society.

8

Chapter 8: The Legacy of Wealth

For many billionaires, the legacy they leave behind is of paramount importance. This chapter explores the ways in which the ultra-rich plan and shape their legacies, from philanthropic endeavors to business achievements. It examines the motivations behind legacy-building and the impact of their actions on future generations.

The desire to leave a lasting legacy is a common theme among billionaires. This chapter highlights the various ways in which they strive to make a meaningful impact on the world, from funding educational institutions to creating enduring brands. It also explores the challenges they face in ensuring that their legacies align with their values and the potential for unintended consequences.

Through a series of compelling stories and examples, readers gain insight into the legacy-building efforts of billionaires. The chapter also examines the role of family and the ways in which the ultra-rich involve their loved ones in their legacy plans. From intergenerational wealth transfer to philanthropic initiatives, the legacy of wealth is a multifaceted and evolving concept.

Ultimately, this chapter encourages readers to reflect on their own legacies and the impact they hope to make in the world. It highlights the importance of intentionality and purpose in legacy-building and the potential for creating lasting change through thoughtful and ethical actions.

9

Chapter 9: The Burden of Wealth

While wealth brings many opportunities, it also comes with its own set of challenges and burdens. This chapter delves into the pressures and expectations that come with immense wealth, exploring how billionaires navigate the complexities of their financial responsibilities. It examines the impact of wealth on personal relationships, mental health, and overall well-being.

The burden of wealth is often underestimated, with many assuming that money solves all problems. This chapter highlights the various ways in which billionaires experience the weight of their financial responsibilities, from managing large-scale investments to dealing with the expectations of others. It also explores the impact of wealth on personal relationships, including the challenges of maintaining genuine connections and the potential for isolation.

Through personal anecdotes and interviews, readers gain insight into the emotional and psychological toll of immense wealth. The chapter also examines the coping mechanisms used by billionaires to manage the pressures of their financial responsibilities. From seeking professional advice to practicing mindfulness, the ultra-rich find various ways to navigate the complexities of their wealth.

10

Chapter 10: The Role of Innovation

Innovation is a driving force behind the success of many billionaires, pushing the boundaries of what is possible and transforming industries. This chapter explores the role of innovation in the lives of the ultra-rich, examining how they foster creativity and drive progress. It delves into the challenges and rewards of pioneering new ideas and the impact of innovation on society.

Billionaires often thrive on the cutting edge of technology and business, constantly seeking new ways to disrupt the status quo. This chapter highlights the various ways in which they drive innovation, from investing in startups to leading research and development efforts. It also explores the challenges they face in staying ahead of the competition and the risks involved in pursuing groundbreaking ideas.

Through case studies and interviews, readers gain insight into the mindset and strategies of innovative billionaires. The chapter also examines the role of failure and resilience in the innovation process, highlighting the importance of learning from setbacks and persisting in the face of adversity. From groundbreaking technologies to revolutionary business models, the ultra-rich have the potential to change the world through their innovative efforts.

Ultimately, this chapter encourages readers to embrace a mindset of innovation and creativity in their own lives. It challenges them to think outside the box and explore new possibilities, regardless of their financial resources. By fostering a spirit of innovation, readers can contribute to progress and drive positive change in their own communities.

11

Chapter 11: The Power of Networks

In the world of billionaires, relationships and networks play a crucial role in achieving success and maintaining influence. This chapter explores the importance of social and professional networks in the lives of the ultra-rich, examining how they build and leverage connections to advance their goals. It delves into the dynamics of networking and the impact of relationships on business and personal success.

Billionaires often rely on a vast network of contacts and collaborators to achieve their objectives. This chapter highlights the various ways in which they build and maintain these relationships, from attending exclusive events to participating in industry associations. It also explores the challenges of navigating complex social dynamics and the importance of trust and reciprocity in successful networking.

Through personal anecdotes and examples, readers gain insight into the networking strategies of billionaires and the role of relationships in their success. The chapter also examines the impact of social capital on business opportunities and the ways in which the ultra-rich use their networks to drive change and achieve their goals. From mentorship to collaboration, relationships play a critical role in the lives of billionaires.

Ultimately, this chapter encourages readers to reflect on the power of their own networks and the importance of cultivating meaningful connections. It challenges them to consider how they can leverage their relationships to achieve their goals and make a positive impact in their own lives. By building strong and supportive networks, readers can enhance their personal and professional success.

12

Chapter 12: The Art of Delegation

Delegation is a key skill for billionaires, allowing them to manage their vast responsibilities and focus on their most important tasks. This chapter explores the art of delegation, examining how the ultra-rich build and manage teams to achieve their objectives. It delves into the challenges and benefits of effective delegation and the impact on personal and business success.

Billionaires often oversee large organizations and complex projects, requiring them to delegate tasks and responsibilities to trusted team members. This chapter highlights the various ways in which they build and lead high-performing teams, from hiring top talent to fostering a culture of collaboration and accountability. It also explores the challenges of letting go of control and trusting others to execute their vision.

Through case studies and interviews, readers gain insight into the delegation strategies of successful billionaires. The chapter also examines the role of leadership and communication in effective delegation, highlighting the importance of clear expectations and regular feedback. From empowering team members to managing conflicts, billionaires use delegation as a tool to drive success and achieve their goals.

Ultimately, this chapter encourages readers to reflect on their own delegation skills and the importance of trusting others to help achieve their objectives. It challenges them to consider how they can build and lead high-performing teams in their own lives and the impact of effective delegation on personal and professional success.

13

Chapter 13: The Intersection of Wealth and Politics

The relationship between wealth and politics is a complex and often controversial one. This chapter explores the ways in which billionaires navigate the political landscape, examining how they influence policies and advocate for their interests. It delves into the ethical considerations and the impact of political involvement on society.

Billionaires often have the resources and connections to influence political decisions and shape public policies. This chapter highlights the various ways in which they engage in the political process, from funding campaigns to lobbying for favorable legislation. It also explores the challenges and criticisms they face, including accusations of undue influence and conflicts of interest.

Through case studies and interviews, readers gain insight into the political strategies of billionaires and the impact of their involvement on society. The chapter also examines the role of corporate political activities and the ways in which businesses use their resources to advocate for their interests. From campaign contributions to grassroots advocacy, the intersection of wealth and politics is a multifaceted and evolving landscape.

Ultimately, this chapter encourages readers to reflect on the role of wealth in the political process and the responsibilities that come with political involvement. It challenges them to consider the ethical implications of their own political activities and the importance of advocating for the greater good.

14

Chapter 14: The Balancing Act

Billionaires often find themselves juggling multiple roles and responsibilities, from managing vast business empires to fulfilling personal and family obligations. This chapter explores the balancing act required to navigate these various aspects of their lives, examining the strategies and sacrifices involved. It delves into the challenges of maintaining work-life balance and the impact on their overall well-being.

The demands of managing immense wealth and influence can be overwhelming, requiring billionaires to make difficult choices and prioritize their time and energy. This chapter highlights the various ways in which the ultra-rich attempt to achieve balance, from setting boundaries to delegating responsibilities. It also explores the personal sacrifices they make, including time away from family and the potential for burnout.

Through personal anecdotes and interviews, readers gain insight into the daily routines and practices of billionaires as they strive to balance their professional and personal lives. The chapter also examines the role of self-care and the importance of mental and physical well-being in achieving balance. From exercise and mindfulness practices to spending quality time with loved ones, billionaires employ various strategies to maintain equilibrium.

Ultimately, this chapter encourages readers to reflect on their own work-life balance and the importance of prioritizing their well-being. It challenges them to consider how they can create a more balanced and fulfilling life, regardless of their financial status.

15

Chapter 15: The Influence of Technology

Technology plays a significant role in the lives of billionaires, shaping their businesses, lifestyles, and the way they interact with the world. This chapter explores the impact of technology on the ultra-rich, examining how they harness its power to drive innovation and maintain their competitive edge. It delves into the challenges and opportunities presented by technological advancements and the ethical considerations involved.

Billionaires often have access to cutting-edge technologies and the resources to invest in groundbreaking innovations. This chapter highlights the various ways in which they leverage technology to achieve their goals, from artificial intelligence and automation to digital platforms and cybersecurity. It also explores the challenges of staying ahead in a rapidly evolving tech landscape and the risks associated with technological disruption.

Through case studies and interviews, readers gain insight into the technological strategies of billionaires and the ways in which they integrate technology into their personal and professional lives. The chapter also examines the ethical considerations of technological advancements, including issues of privacy, security, and the digital divide. From data ethics to the impact of automation on jobs, billionaires must navigate complex ethical dilemmas in their pursuit of progress.

Ultimately, this chapter encourages readers to reflect on the role of technology in their own lives and the importance of ethical decision-making in the digital age. It challenges them to consider how they can harness the power of technology for positive change while addressing the ethical implications of their actions.

16

Chapter 16: The Dynamics of Family Wealth

Family plays a crucial role in the lives of billionaires, influencing their decisions and shaping their legacies. This chapter explores the dynamics of family wealth, examining how the ultra-rich navigate issues of inheritance, succession, and intergenerational relationships. It delves into the challenges and complexities of maintaining family harmony and the impact on their personal and professional lives.

The transfer of wealth from one generation to the next is a significant concern for billionaires, requiring careful planning and consideration. This chapter highlights the various ways in which the ultra-rich approach inheritance and succession, from creating trusts and foundations to involving their children in business ventures. It also explores the challenges of managing family dynamics and the potential for conflict and division.

Through personal anecdotes and interviews, readers gain insight into the family dynamics of billionaires and the strategies they use to maintain harmony and unity. The chapter also examines the role of education and mentorship in preparing the next generation for their responsibilities. From fostering a sense of purpose and values to providing opportunities for growth and development, billionaires invest in their families to ensure a lasting legacy.

Ultimately, this chapter encourages readers to reflect on the importance of family relationships and the impact of wealth on their own lives. It challenges them to consider how they can create a positive and supportive family environment and the potential for building a lasting legacy through thoughtful and intentional actions.

17

Chapter 17: The Future of Wealth

As the world continues to evolve, the concept of wealth and its role in society is constantly changing. This chapter explores the future of wealth, examining the trends and challenges that will shape the lives of billionaires in the years to come. It delves into the potential for new forms of wealth creation and the impact of global economic and social shifts.

The future of wealth is likely to be influenced by a variety of factors, including technological advancements, environmental concerns, and changing social norms. This chapter highlights the emerging trends and challenges that billionaires will need to navigate, from the rise of digital currencies and sustainable investing to the increasing demand for social responsibility and transparency. It also explores the potential for new opportunities and the ways in which the ultra-rich can adapt to these changes.

Through a forward-looking perspective, readers gain insight into the potential future landscape of wealth and the strategies that billionaires may employ to stay ahead. The chapter also examines the role of innovation and adaptability in navigating an uncertain future, highlighting the importance of foresight and resilience. From embracing new technologies to addressing global challenges, billionaires have the potential to drive positive change and shape the future of society.

Ultimately, this chapter encourages readers to consider the future of wealth and their own role in shaping it. It challenges them to think about the impact of their actions on future generations and the potential for creating a more equitable and sustainable world. By understanding the trends and challenges that lie ahead, readers can prepare for the future and contribute to a better, more inclusive society.

The Weight of Wealth: How Billionaires Navigate Power, Purpose, and Humanity

In a world where the ultra-rich wield unparalleled influence, "The Weight of Wealth" delves deep into the lives of billionaires as they navigate the complex terrain of power, purpose, and humanity. This captivating book takes readers on an intimate journey, exploring the multifaceted experiences of the super-wealthy and the profound impact of their actions on society.

Through a series of compelling chapters, the book examines the delicate balance between wielding immense power and maintaining ethical integrity. It highlights the purposeful endeavors of billionaires who channel their wealth towards philanthropy and social change, while also shedding light on the personal struggles and emotional toll that come with such immense responsibilities.

Readers are offered a rare glimpse into the human side of the ultra-rich, revealing the challenges they face in building

www.ingramcontent.com/pod-product-compliance
Lightning Source LLC
LaVergne TN
LVHW020739090526
838202LV00057BA/6087